Be More Brontë

Be More Brontë

Words of wisdom from the world's most famous sisters

CICO BOOKS

Published in 2026 by CICO Books

An imprint of Ryland Peters & Small Ltd
20–21 Jockey's Fields
London WC1R 4BW
1452 Davis Bugg Road
Warrenton, NC 27589
www.rylandpeters.com
Email: euregulations@rylandpeters.com

10 9 8 7 6 5 4 3 2 1

See page 144 for picture credits.

A CIP record for this book is available from the British Library.
US Library of Congress CIP data has been applied for.

ISBN: 978 1 80065 575 1

Printed in China

In-house editor: Jenny Dye
Designer: Geoff Borin
Art director: Sally Powell
Creative director: Leslie Harrington
Head of production: Patricia Harrington
Publishing manager: Carmel Edmonds

The authorised representative in the EEA is
Authorised Rep Compliance Ltd., Ground Floor.
71 Lower Baggot Street, Dublin, D01 P593, Ireland
www.arccompliance.com

FSC www.fsc.org
MIX
Paper | Supporting responsible forestry
FSC® C106563

Contents

Introduction

Powerful and strikingly original, the Brontës' novels and poetry continue to provide endless inspiration.

Born in the early 1800s, Charlotte, Emily, and Anne, together with their brother Branwell, grew up in Haworth, West Yorkshire, on the edge of the moors. Tragically, their mother passed away when the siblings were still children and their two older sisters, Maria and Elizabeth, died from tuberculosis at just 10 and 11 years old while at school.

Their father, Patrick Brontë, encouraged his daughters' education, and their love of writing began in childhood. They created imaginary worlds and wrote about them in tiny handmade books.

Charlotte, Emily, and Anne's passion for writing stories and poetry continued throughout their lives. By 1846, they had succeeded in publishing a book of poems under the pseudonyms Currer, Ellis, and Acton Bell, as women weren't expected to be writers at the time.

Many of the central female characters of their novels challenged societal expectations and sought self-reliance, so in this book you'll find empowering quotations on independence from the sisters' groundbreaking writing. You'll also discover haunting words on the power of nature, inspired by the wild and untamed landscape of the Yorkshire moors where the Brontës lived.

Experience the passion of the sisters' novels with captivating lines from their characters who pursued romantic love, sometimes overturning convention through unusual partnerships. Solidarity through platonic relationships is valued too, so find strength in their words on female friendship and sisterly bonds. And finally, gain wisdom and solace about enduring hardships and overcoming challenges.

Whether you are looking for inspiration, guidance, or comfort, or you want to use the lines as a stepping-off point for exploring more of the Brontës' works, this beautiful book of quotations is perfect for keeping close to hand.

Charlotte Brontë (1816–1855)

In 1847, Charlotte's novel *Jane Eyre* was published and became an instant success. One of the most powerful romances ever written, it follows the story of a fiercely independent young woman who pursues love on her own terms and finds a dark secret in the home of her employer Mr. Rochester.

Shirley, published in 1849, is set in a time of social and political unrest in an industrializing Yorkshire. It explores the friendship between its two protagonists, Shirley Keeldar and Caroline Helstone, and tells their two love stories.

Published in 1853, *Villette* was inspired by Charlotte's time as a student in Brussels. It centers around Lucy Snowe as she navigates loneliness, love, and independence in her new life in Villette, France where she is a teacher at a girls' boarding school.

The Professor was the first novel Charlotte wrote and it was published in 1857 after her death. Also inspired by her time in Brussels, the novel follows William Crimsworth as he leaves a cheerless clerkship in industrial Yorkshire and becomes a teacher in Belgium.

Emily Brontë (1818–1848)

A turbulent story of obsessive passion, Emily's only novel *Wuthering Heights* shocked readers and critics when it was published in 1847. Catherine Earnshaw is torn between wealthy and aristocratic Edgar Linton and Heathcliff, a foundling who was taken into the Earnshaw family and became close to Catherine from childhood. The intense relationships between the families stir up a bitterness and cruelty that haunt the lives of the children of the next generation, Cathy Linton and Linton Heathcliff.

Anne Brontë (1820–1849)

Based on her own experience of finding work as a woman in the 19th century, Anne's first novel, *Agnes Grey*, was published in 1847. After her family falls on hard times, Agnes is determined to prove herself and earn a living as a governess. The novel follows her struggles and successes as she finds her own way in life.

Her second novel, *The Tenant of Wildfell Hall*, was published one year later in 1848, and tells the story of its heroine Helen Huntingdon, the mysterious young widow who is the new tenant at Wildfell Hall, and her brave escape from her alcoholic and abusive husband.

Chapter 1

Courage & Independence

"I am no bird; and no net ensnares me; I am a free human being with an independent will, which I now exert to leave you."

Charlotte Brontë, *Jane Eyre*

Jane, to Mr. Rochester

"I am anchored on a resolve you cannot shake. My heart, my conscience ſhall dispose of my hand – they only. Know this at last."

Charlotte Brontë, *Shirley*

Shirley Keeldar, to Mr. Sympson

"How delightful it would be to be a governess! To go out into the world; to enter upon a new life; to act for myself; to exercise my unused faculties; to try my unknown powers; to earn my own maintenance..."

Anne Brontë, *Agnes Grey*

Agnes, considering her future

"I remembered that the real world was wide, and that a varied field of hopes and fears, of sensations and excitements, awaited those who had the courage to go forth into its expanse, to seek real knowledge of life amidst its perils."

Charlotte Brontë, *Jane Eyre*

Jane, while at Lowood school

"I'll walk where my own nature would be leading: It vexes me to choose another guide:

Where the grey flocks in
ferny glens are feeding;
Where the wild wind blows
on the mountain side."

Emily Brontë, "Stanzas"

"One bright day in the last week of February, I was walking in the park, enjoying the threefold luxury of solitude, a book, and pleasant weather."

Anne Brontë, *Agnes Grey*

Agnes, during her time as a governess at Horton Lodge

"I am now quite cured of seeking pleasure in society, be it country or town. A sensible man ought to find sufficient company in himself."

Emily Brontë, *Wuthering Heights*

Mr. Lockwood, to Heathcliff

"'I am not an angel,' I asserted; 'and I will not be one till I die: I will be myself. Mr. Rochester, you must neither expect nor exact anything celestial of me – for you will not get it, any more than I shall get it of you: which I do not at all anticipate.'"

Charlotte Brontë, *Jane Eyre*

Jane, to Mr. Rochester

"I maintain that, if she were more perfect, she would be less interesting."

Anne Brontë, *The Tenant of Wildfell Hall*

Gilbert Markham, on Eliza Millward

"Do not be over-persuaded to marry a man you can never respect – I do not say love, because, I think, if you can respect a person before marriage, moderate love at least will come after; and as to intense passion, I am convinced that this is no desirable feeling."

Charlotte Brontë, in a letter to her friend Ellen Nussey; Haworth, May 15, 1840

"If life be a war, it seemed my destiny to conduct it single-handed."

Charlotte Brontë, *Villette*

Lucy Snowe

"I can live alone, if self-respect, and circumstances require me so to do. I need not sell my soul to buy bliss. I have an inward treasure born with me, which can keep me alive if all extraneous delights should be withheld, or offered only at a price I cannot afford to give."

Charlotte Brontë, *Jane Eyre*

Mr. Rochester, while disguised as a gypsy, describing Jane's character

"No coward soul is mine,
No trembler in the world's
storm-troubled sphere,

I see Heaven's glories shine
And Faith shines equal,
arming me from Fear"

Emily Brontë, "No Coward Soul is Mine"

"When I tell you not to marry without love, I do not advise you to marry for love alone: there are many, many other things to be considered. Keep both heart and hand in your own possession, till you see good reason to part with them; and if such an occasion should never present itself, comfort your mind with this reflection, that though in single life your joys may not be very many, your sorrows, at least, will not be more than you can bear. Marriage may change your circumstances for the better, but, in my private opinion, it is far more likely to produce a contrary result."

Anne Brontë, *The Tenant of Wildfell Hall*

Mrs. Huntingdon, advising Esther Hargrave

"The thing that irks me most is this shattered prison, after all. I'm tired, tired of being enclosed here. I'm wearying to escape into that glorious world, and to be always there; not seeing it dimly through tears, and yearning for it through the walls of an aching heart; but really with it, and in it."

Emily Brontë, *Wuthering Heights*

Catherine, to Nelly Dean

"Do you think, because I am poor, obscure, plain, and little, I am soulless and heartless? You think wrong! – I have as much soul as you – and full as much heart! And if God had gifted me with some beauty and much wealth, I should have made it as hard for you to leave me, as it is now for me to leave you. I am not talking to you now through the medium of custom, conventionalities, nor even of mortal flesh; – it is my spirit that addresses your spirit; just as if both had passed through the grave, and we stood at God's feet, equal – as we are!"

Charlotte Brontë, *Jane Eyre*

Jane, to Mr. Rochester

"Women are supposed to be very calm generally: but women feel just as men feel; they need exercise for their faculties, and a field for their efforts as much as their brothers do; they suffer from too rigid a restraint, too absolute a stagnation, precisely as men would suffer..."

Charlotte Brontë, *Jane Eyre*

Jane, during her first few weeks at Thornfield

"Come what may afterwards, an education secured is an advantage gained – a priceless advantage. Come what may – it is a step towards independence – and one great curse of a single female life is its dependency."

Charlotte Brontë, in a letter to William Smith Williams; Haworth, July 3, 1849

"I care for myself.
The more solitary, the
more friendless, the more
unsustained I am, the more
I will respect myself."

Charlotte Brontë, *Jane Eyre*

Jane, to Mr. Rochester

"She's hard to guide any way but her own."

Emily Brontë, *Wuthering Heights*

Nelly Dean, on Catherine

Chapter 2

The Power of Nature

"I wish I were a girl again, half savage and hardy, and free...

Why am I so changed?...

I'm sure I should be myself were I once among the heather on those hills."

Emily Brontë, *Wuthering Heights*

Catherine

"A fine and subtle
spirit dwells,
In every little flower,
Each one its own sweet
feeling breathes,
With more or less
of power.

There is a silent eloquence
In every wild bluebell,
That fills my softened
heart with bliss,
That words could
never tell."

Anne Brontë, "The Bluebell"

"Spring drew on ... and a greenness grew over those brown beds, which, freshening daily, suggested the thought that Hope traversed them at night, and left each morning brighter traces of her steps."

Charlotte Brontë, *Jane Eyre*

Jane, while at Lowood school

"It was not without a certain wild pleasure I ran before the wind, delivering my trouble of mind to the measureless air-torrent thundering through space."

Charlotte Brontë, *Jane Eyre*

Jane, before her wedding day

"I touched the heath: it was dry, and yet warm with the heat of the summer day. I looked at the sky; it was pure: a kindly star twinkled just above the chasm ridge.

The dew fell, but with propitious softness; no breeze whispered. Nature seemed to me benign and good; I thought she loved me, outcast as I was..."

Charlotte Brontë, *Jane Eyre*

Jane, after leaving Thornfield

"My soul is awakened,
my spirit is soaring,
And carried aloft on
the winds of the breeze;

For above and around me the wild wind is roaring, Arousing to rapture the earth and the seas."

Anne Brontë, "Lines Composed in a Wood on a Windy Day"

"In winter nothing more dreary, in summer nothing more divine, than those glens shut in by hills, and those bluff, bold swells of heath."

Emily Brontë, *Wuthering Heights*

Mr. Lockwood, describing the Yorkshire moors

"I will stay out here with my mother Eve, in these days called Nature. I love her – undying, mighty being! Heaven may have faded from her brow when she fell in paradise, but all that is glorious on earth shines there still."

Charlotte Brontë, *Shirley*

Shirley Keeldar, telling Caroline Helstone that she will not go into church

'I lingered round them,
under that benign sky;
watched the moths
fluttering among the heath
and hare-bells; listened
to the soft wind breathing
through the grass;

and wondered how anyone could ever imagine unquiet slumbers for the sleepers in that quiet earth."

Emily Brontë, *Wuthering Heights*

Mr. Lockwood, contemplating the graves of Linton, Heathcliff, and Catherine

"He said the pleasantest manner of spending a hot July day was lying from morning till evening on a bank of heath in the middle of the moors ... the blue sky and bright sun shining steadily and cloudlessly. That was his most perfect idea of heaven's happiness: mine was rocking in a rustling green tree, with a west wind blowing, and bright white clouds flitting rapidly above; and not only larks, but throstles, and blackbirds, and linnets, and cuckoos pouring out music on every side, and the moors seen at a distance, broken into cool dusky dells; but close by great swells of long grass undulating in waves to the breeze; and woods and sounding water, and the whole world awake and wild with joy."

Emily Brontë, *Wuthering Heights*

Cathy Linton, on a disagreement with Linton Heathcliff

"Every leaf
speaks bliss to me,
Fluttering from the
autumn tree."

Emily Brontë, "Fall, leaves, fall"

"This is a terrible hour, but it is often that darkest point which precedes the rise of day; that turn of the year when the icy January wind carries over the waste at once the dirge of departing winter, and the prophecy of coming spring."

Charlotte Brontë, *Shirley*

'Awaken on all
my dear moorlands,
The wind in its glory
and pride!

O call me from valleys and highlands,
To walk by the hill-river's side!"

Emily Brontë, "Loud without the wind was roaring"

Chapter 3

Romantic Love

"...he's more myself than I am. Whatever our souls are made of, his and mine are the same..."

Emily Brontë, *Wuthering Heights*

Catherine, on Heathcliff

"Catherine, you know that I could as soon forget you, as my existence!"

Emily Brontë, *Wuthering Heights*

Heathcliff, to Catherine

"I am strangely glad to get back again to you; and wherever you are is my home – my only home."

Charlotte Brontë, *Jane Eyre*

Jane, to Mr. Rochester

"First study; then approve; then love. Let your eyes be blind to all external attractions, your ears deaf to all the fascinations of flattery and light discourse... If you should marry the handsomest, and most accomplished and superficially agreeable man in the world, you little know the misery that would overwhelm you if, after all, you should find him to be a worthless reprobate, or even an impracticable fool."

Anne Brontë, *The Tenant of Wildfell Hall*

Mrs. Maxwell, advising her niece Helen Huntingdon

"That to begin with; let respect be the foundation, affection the first floor, love the superstructure..."

Charlotte Brontë, *The Professor*

M. Pelet, to William Crimsworth

"His mind was indeed my library, and whenever it was opened to me, I entered bliss."

Charlotte Brontë, *Villette*

Lucy Snowe, on M. Paul Emanuel

"If all else perished, and he remained, I should still continue to be; and if all else remained, and he were annihilated, the Universe would turn to a mighty stranger."

Emily Brontë, *Wuthering Heights*

Catherine, on Heathcliff

"Every atom of your flesh is as dear to me as my own: in pain and sickness it would still be dear. Your mind is my treasure, and if it were broken, it would be my treasure still..."

Charlotte Brontë, *Jane Eyre*

Mr. Rochester, to Jane

"My love for Linton is like the foliage in the woods. Time will change it, I'm well aware, as winter changes the trees – my love for Heathcliff resembles the eternal rocks beneath – a source of little visible delight, but necessary."

Emily Brontë, *Wuthering Heights*

Catherine, on Edgar Linton and Heathcliff

"All my heart is yours, sir: it belongs to you; and with you it would remain, were fate to exile the rest of me from your presence for ever."

Charlotte Brontë, *Jane Eyre*

Jane, to Mr. Rochester

"I ask you to pass through life at my side – to be my second self, and best earthly companion."

Charlotte Brontë, *Jane Eyre*

Mr. Rochester, to Jane

"Nelly, I *am* Heathcliff – he's always, always in my mind – not as a pleasure, any more than I am always a pleasure to myself, but as my own being."

Emily Brontë, *Wuthering Heights*

Catherine, on Heathcliff

"Two words would comprehend my future – *death* and *hell* – existence, after losing her, would be hell.

Yet I was a fool to fancy for a moment that she valued Edgar Linton's attachment more than mine – If he loved with all the powers of his puny being, he couldn't love as much in eighty years, as I could in a day. And Catherine has a heart as deep as I have; the sea could be as readily contained in that horse-trough, as her whole affection be monopolized by him."

Emily Brontë, *Wuthering Heights*

Heathcliff, to Nelly Dean

"I have for the first time found what I can truly love – I have found *you*. You are my sympathy – my better self – my good angel. I am bound to you with a strong attachment. I think you good, gifted, lovely: a fervent, a solemn passion is conceived in my heart; it leans to you, draws you to my centre and spring of life, wraps my existence about you, and, kindling in pure, powerful flame, fuses you and me in one."

Charlotte Brontë, *Jane Eyre*

Mr. Rochester, to Jane

"My great miseries
in this world have been Heathcliff's
miseries, and I watched and felt each
from the beginning; my great thought
in living is himself."

Emily Brontë, *Wuthering Heights*

Catherine, to Nelly Dean

"You – you strange,
you almost unearthly thing! –
I love as my own flesh.
You – poor and obscure,
and small and plain as you
are – I entreat to accept
me as a husband."

Charlotte Brontë, *Jane Eyre*

Mr. Rochester, to Jane

"*Why* did you betray your own heart, Cathy? ... You loved me – then what *right* had you to leave me? ... I have not broken your heart – *you* have broken it – and in breaking it, you have broken mine ... Do I want to live? What kind of living will it be when you – oh, God! Would *you* like to live with your soul in the grave?"

Emily Brontë, *Wuthering Heights*

Heathcliff, to Catherine

"I sometimes have a queer feeling with regard to you – especially when you are near me, as now: it is as if I had a string somewhere under my left ribs, tightly and inextricably knotted to a similar string situated in the corresponding quarter of your little frame."

Charlotte Brontë, *Jane Eyre*

Mr. Rochester, to Jane

"He had not breathed a word of love, or dropped one hint of tenderness or affection, and yet I had been supremely happy. To be near him, to hear him talk ... as he did talk;

and to feel that he thought me worthy to be spoken to ... capable of understanding and duly appreciating such discourse ... was enough."

Anne Brontë, *Agnes Grey*

Agnes, on Edward Weston

"I know what it is to
live entirely for and with
what I love best on earth.
I hold myself supremely blest
– blest beyond what language
can express; because I am my
husband's life as fully
as he is mine."

Charlotte Brontë, *Jane Eyre*

Jane, on Mr. Rochester

"One glance he gave, one little smile at parting – it was but for a moment; but therein I read, or thought I read, a meaning that kindled in my heart a brighter flame of hope than had ever yet arisen."

Anne Brontë, *Agnes Grey*

Agnes, on Edward Weston

"For what is not connected with her to me? and what does not recall her? I cannot look down to this floor, but her features are shaped in the flags! In every cloud, in every tree – filling the air at night, and caught by glimpses in every object, by day I am surrounded with her image! ... The entire world is a dreadful collection of memoranda that she did exist, and that I have lost her!"

Emily Brontë, *Wuthering Heights*

Heathcliff, on Catherine

"I turned my lips to the hand that lay on my shoulder. I loved him very much – more than I could trust myself to say – more than words had power to express."

Charlotte Brontë, *Jane Eyre*

Jane, on Mr. Rochester

"Love is real – the most real, the most lasting, the sweetest and yet the bitterest thing we know."

Charlotte Brontë, *Shirley*

Caroline Helstone, to Mrs. Pryor

"Some have won
a wild delight,
By daring wilder sorrow;
Could I gain thy
love to-night,
I'd hazard death
to-morrow."

Charlotte Brontë, "Passion"

"Catherine Earnshaw, may you not rest, as long as I am living! You said I killed you – haunt me then ... I believe – I know that! Ghosts have wandered on earth. Be with me always

– take any form – drive me mad! Only do not leave me in this abyss, where I cannot find you! Oh, God! it is unutterable! I cannot live without my life! I cannot live without my soul!"

Emily Brontë, *Wuthering Heights*

Heathcliff, on the death of Catherine

"I shall never forget that glorious summer evening, and always remember with delight that steep, rugged hill, and the edge of the precipice where we stood together watching the splendid sun-set mirrored on the restless world of waters at our feet – with hearts filled with gratitude to Heaven, and happiness, and love – almost too full for speech."

Anne Brontë, *Agnes Grey*

Agnes, on her engagement to Edward Weston

"There is such a thing as looking through a person's eyes into the heart, and learning more of the height, and breadth, and depth of another's soul in one hour, than it might take you a life time to discover, if he or she were not disposed to reveal it – or if you had not the sense to understand it."

Anne Brontë, *The Tenant of Wildfell Hall*

Gilbert Markham, on Helen Graham

"Reader,
I married him."

Charlotte Brontë, *Jane Eyre*

Jane, on Mr. Rochester

Chapter 4

Family & Friendship

"There is no happiness like that of being loved by your fellow-creatures, and feeling that your presence is an addition to their comfort."

Charlotte Brontë, *Jane Eyre*

Jane, on returning to Thornfield after the funeral of her aunt, Mrs. Reed

"I think Emily seems the nearest thing to my heart in this world."

Charlotte Brontë, on her sister Emily,
in a letter to her friend Ellen Nussey;
Haworth, November 23, 1848

'Love is like the
wild rose briar,
Friendship, like the
holly-tree,

The holly is dark when
the rose briar blooms,
But which will bloom
most constantly?

Emily Brontë, "Love is like the wild rose briar"

"Though I am a defective being, with many faults and few redeeming points, yet I never tired of Helen Burns; nor ever ceased to cherish for her a sentiment of attachment, as strong, tender, and respectful as any that ever animated my heart. How could it be otherwise, when Helen, at all times and under all circumstances, evinced for me a quiet and faithful friendship, which ill-humour never soured, nor irritation ever troubled?"

Charlotte Brontë, *Jane Eyre*

Jane, on her friend Helen Burns, while at Lowood school

"Oh, that lone flower
recalled to me,
My happy
childhood's hours,
When bluebells seemed
like fairy gifts,
A prize among
the flowers.

Those sunny days
of merriment,
When heart and
soul were free,
And when I dwelt
with kindred hearts,
That loved and
cared for me."

Anne Brontë, "The Bluebell"

"Friendship ... is a plant which cannot be forced – true friendship is no gourd springing up in a night and withering in a day. When I first saw Ellen I did not care for her – we were schoolfellows – in the course of time we learnt each others [sic] faults and good points – we were contrasts –

still we suited – affection was first a germ, then a sapling – then a strong tree: now – no new friend, however lofty or profound in intellect ... could be to me what Ellen is ... she is good – she is true – she is faithful and I love her."

Charlotte Brontë, on her friend Ellen Nussey, in a letter to William Smith Williams; Haworth, January 3, 1850

"Shirley, I never had a sister – you never had a sister; but it flashes on me at this moment how sisters feel towards each other – affection twined with their life, which no shocks of feeling can uproot, which little quarrels only trample an instant, that it may spring more freshly when the pressure is removed; affection that no passion can ultimately outrival, with which even love itself cannot do more than compete in force and truth."

Charlotte Brontë, *Shirley*

Caroline Helstone, to Shirley Keeldar

"Now, as I watch
that distant hill,
So faint, so blue,
so far removed,

Sweet dreams of home
my heart may fill,
That home where I am
known and loved."

Charlotte Brontë, "The Teacher's Monologue"

"If all the world hated you, and believed you wicked, while your own conscience approved you, and absolved you from guilt, you would not be without friends."

Charlotte Brontë, *Jane Eyre*

Helen Burns, to Jane

"When she [Emily] is ill there seems to be no sunshine in the world for me; the tie of sister is near and dear indeed, and I think a certain harshness in her powerful and peculiar character only makes me cling to her more."

Charlotte Brontë, in a letter to William Smith Williams; Haworth, 2 November 1848

Chapter 5

Trials & Resilience

"I believe in some blending of hope and sunshine sweetening the worst lots. I believe that this life is not all; neither the beginning nor the end. I believe while I tremble; I trust while I weep."

Charlotte Brontë, *Villette*

Lucy Snowe

"The ties that bind us to life are tougher than you imagine, or than any one can, who has not felt how roughly they may be pulled without breaking."

Anne Brontë, *Agnes Grey*

Edward Weston, to Agnes

"What matters it,
that, all around
Danger, and guilt,
and darkness lie,
If but within our
bosom's bound

We hold a bright,
untroubled sky,
Warm with ten thousand
mingled rays
Of suns that know
no winter days?”

Emily Brontë, “To Imagination”

"In sunshine, in prosperity, the flowers are very well; but how many wet days are there in life – November seasons of disaster, when a man's hearth and home would be cold indeed, without the clear, cheering gleam of intellect."

Charlotte Brontë, *The Professor*

William Crimsworth

"Well, there's nothing like active employment, I suppose, to console the afflicted."

Anne Brontë, *The Tenant of Wildfell Hall*

Eliza Millward, to Gilbert Markham

"I believe, in my heart, we were intended to prize life and enjoy it, so long as we retain it. Existence never was originally meant to be that useless, blank, pale, slow-trailing thing it often becomes to many, and is becoming to me, among the rest."

Charlotte Brontë, *Shirley*

Caroline Helstone

"Time brought resignation, and a melancholy sweeter than common joy."

Emily Brontë, *Wuthering Heights*

Nelly Dean, describing Edgar Linton after the death of his wife Catherine

"Renewing, then, my courage, and gathering my feeble remains of strength, I pushed on."

Charlotte Brontë, *Jane Eyre*

Jane, after leaving Thornfield

"To see and know the worst is to take from Fear her main advantage."

Charlotte Brontë, *Villette*

Lucy Snowe

"Life appears to me too short to be spent in nursing animosity, or registering wrongs."

Charlotte Brontë, *Jane Eyre*

Helen Burns, to Jane

"But if I feel, may I *never* express?"

"Never!" declared Reason... This hag, this Reason, would not let me look up, or smile, or hope: she could not rest unless I were altogether crushed, cowed, broken-in, and broken down... Reason might be right; yet no wonder we are glad at times to defy her, to rush from under her rod and give a truant hour to Imagination – *her* soft, bright foe, *our* sweet Help, our divine Hope."

Charlotte Brontë, *Villette*

Lucy Snowe

"It is foolish to wish for beauty. Sensible people never either desire it for themselves or care about it in others. If the mind be but well cultivated, and the heart well disposed, not one ever cares for the exterior."

Anne Brontë, *Agnes Grey*

Agnes

"That gift of poetry –
the most divine bestowed on
man – was, I believe, granted
to allay emotions when their
strength threatens harm."

Charlotte Brontë, *Shirley*

Caroline Helstone, to Shirley Keeldar

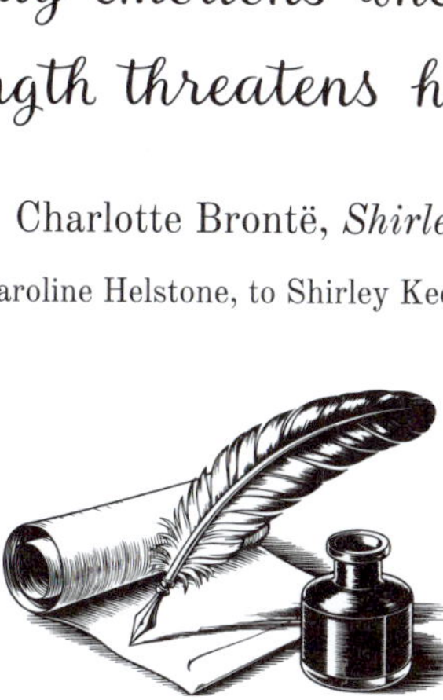

"Our power of being happy lies a good deal in ourselves, I believe."

Charlotte Brontë, *Shirley*

Caroline Helstone, to Shirley Keeldar

"If you would have your son to walk honourably through the world, you must not attempt to clear the stones from his path, but teach him to walk firmly over them – not insist upon leading him by the hand, but let him learn to go alone."

Anne Brontë, *The Tenant of Wildfell Hall*

Gilbert Markham, to Helen Graham

"Cheerfulness, it would appear,
is a matter which depends fully as
much on the state of things within,
as on the state of things without
and around us."

Charlotte Brontë, *Shirley*

"I had been seasoned by adversity, and tutored by experience, and I longed to redeem my lost honour in the eyes of those whose opinion was more than that of all the world to me."

Anne Brontë, *Agnes Grey*

Agnes, after leaving her first position as a governess

"I feel that, as –

'Stone walls do not a prison make,
Nor iron bars – a cage',

so peril, loneliness, an uncertain future, are not oppressive evils, so long as the frame is healthy and the faculties are employed; so long, especially, as Liberty lends us her wings, and Hope guides us by her star."

Charlotte Brontë, *Villette*

Lucy Snowe

"What necessity is there to dwell on the Past, when the Present is so much surer – the Future so much brighter?"

Charlotte Brontë, *Jane Eyre*

Mr. Rochester, to Jane

Picture Credits

Adobe Stock and the following creators: monamonash: motifs on pages 1, 5, 14–15, 18–19, 23, 26–27, 30–31, 36, 40–41, 44, 48–49, 58–59, 65, 66–67, 70–71, 72, 75, 76–77, 82–83, 86–87, 89, 90–91, 98–99, 104, 108–109, 112–113, 116–117, 122–123, 126, 131, 132–133, 138–139, 140, 142–143; **Chandlerlikes:** pages 2–3, 24–25, 62–63; **HiSunnySky:** pages 6–9, 12–13, 16–17, 20–21, 28–29, 34, 37, 42–43, 45, 50–53, 56–57, 64, 68–69, 73–74, 80–81, 84–85, 88, 92–93, 96–97, 100–101, 105–107, 114–115, 118–119, 127, 130, 134–137, 141; **Julia:** pages 10–11, 78–79, 128–129; **sketched-graphics:** page 12 (bird); **ND STOCK:** pages 32–33, 60–61; **javier:** pages 38–39, 94–95; **Imron:** pages 46–47, 110–111, 120–121; **NATASHA-CHU:** page 56 (leaves); **Mariia Mazaeva:** page 69 (book); **Morena:** page 101 (rings); **SagorKundu:** page 137 (quill and ink)